The
Path

Russell Topping

ISBN 979-8-89243-505-5 (paperback)
ISBN 979-8-89243-506-2 (digital)

Christian Faith Publishing
832 Park Avenue
Meadville, PA 16335
www.christianfaithpublishing.com

Printed in the United States of America

Contents

It's Raining Again

It's raining again.
It taps against my windowpane.
I'm lying here
remembering my youth.
Putting on our swimsuits
running carefree through the gutters
laughing loudly
as only a child can laugh.
I can remember
how much simpler life was back then.
I long to go back
because life is so complicated now.

My Wife

She brightened my dreariest days and made my life
    bearable
with her wisdom and loving ways.
Made my existence seem not so terrible
her smile warmed my coldest days.
She warmed the house and my heart with a grace
I did not deserve.
Loving me with everything she had and was, holding
nothing in reserve.
Her nearness comforted me even in my deepest pain
and I rejoice that we will see each other again.

The Sun Rises

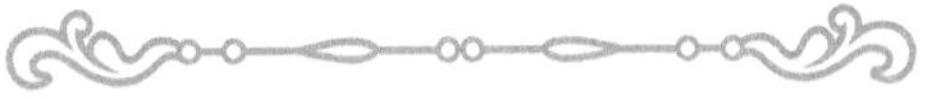

The sun rises
And with it my hopes
Chasing away the darkness

Dreams

Dreams die sacrificed on the altar of necessity
Dreams fade
Like flowers past their prime
Dreams wilt
As the sun of adversity beats down

I Looked into My Soul

I looked into my soul today, and what I saw caused
　　me the deepest fright
for I saw a darkness there, as dark as a winter's night.
It filled my spirit's height, length, and breadth, and
　　from that darkness
a hand reached out to drag me into that dark with a
　　grip so strong and tight.
I looked in my soul today and saw a fire blazing hot
　　and out of control.
I heard its voice drowning out all other sounds, I felt
　　its searing heat
It threatened one man's life and another's mortal soul.
I knew I should run away, I should flee, but its power
　　to hold knew no bounds.
I looked into my soul today and saw myself standing
　　on the shore of anger's sea.
Cold, gray waves broke at my feet, only to run away
　　again.
And as I stood there gazing at the horizon, I felt the
　　urge to plunge into that sea
And swim until I sank beneath the waves.

Just When

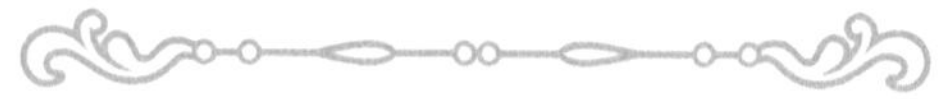

Just when I thought I had all the answers, life went
 and changed the questions,
leaving me at a loss as to what to do.
So I started searching all over again, and that search
 led me to you.
Just when I thought I had it all together and every-
 thing was in order,
you came into my life and turned it upside down.
So I had to step out in faith, and because of that, my
 faith grew by leaps and bounds.
Just when I thought I knew what love was all about,
 you showed me it was about
so much more.
You took away the emptiness that filled my life and
 made life worth living.

Out of the Ashes

Out of the ashes
Of disappointment rises
Like the phoenix, hope

Ineloquent

I struggle to tell you how I feel,
but the words don't come easily
and when they do, they seem so unreal.
I can think of no new words, no matter how hard I try
they've all been said before by those more eloquent
    than I.
So much I want to say that I don't know where to start,
so I'll just have to be content to know you know my
    heart.

Rummaging

Rummaging through the closet of my mind,
I'm not sure exactly what I will find.
Taking off some old thoughts, putting on some new
Hopefully, I'll be a better person by the time I am
through.

Sunrise

Over the jade-green sea
the sun grasps at a brand-new day
with fingers of hot orange

Saturday Night

I'm sitting here in the bar with my head in a funk,
 feelin' lonely and sad,
I'm thinking this must be a dream 'cos life can't be
 this bad.
In walks this this woman, looking tall and fine and cool
and plops herself down on the nearest stool.
I introduced myself with a polite little cough.
She smiled sweetly and told me to shove off.
Right then and there, I knew she'd cause me a great
 deal of strife,
because the way my luck's been running, she's probably
somebody's wife.

On the Death of a Friend

John was buried the other day, he died at forty-three,
Too young, you say, but he was as old as me.
It was cold and windy, rain falling from a sky so gray
and when it came time to speak, no one had very
　　much to say.
And as I watched the final ceremonies, a thought
　　came unbidden to mind,
A thought to which I had previously been blind.
When I am gone and my life not much more than a
　　memory,
As they gather at my grave, what will they say about
　　me?

When I Am Alone with You

When I am alone with you, the world vanishes, and
    I really don't care where it went.
Time slows to a crawl or even stops, and I am
    reminded of what's truly important.
When I am alone with you, I see your beautiful smile,
    all my pain is forgotten.
I find the rest my weary soul needs, and I am sorry
    that our time together must end.
When I am alone with you, my problems fade to
    nothing, and your love fills my weary mind,
I can face the world again, I find the joy I thought
    would never again be mine.

The First Snow

The first snow melted quietly, as had my innocence
and youth.
So quietly, in fact, that I never realized that it had
gone.
That's always the case when you face life's truth.
I guess I knew the first snow would not last.
I know also it's true that none of us can live in the
past.

I've Been Down This Road Before

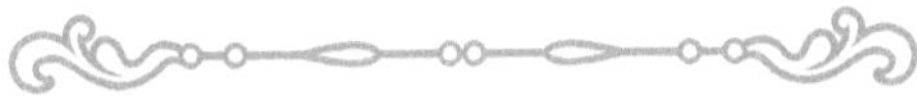

I've been down this road before
A hundred times it seems.
The road of shattered hopes,
the road of broken dreams.
The road with countless twists and turns
that never seems to end, where fear is always
lurking just around the bend.
I've been down this road before.
A road of disappointment and grief.
A road of unshed tears and private pain.
Why I keep on this road, I can never really
Explain.

You Speak

You speak powerful words
and all my fears scatter
like a flock of startled birds.

At Peace

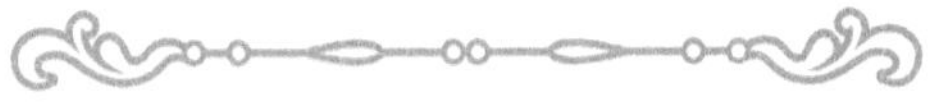

At peace, total peace
is the heart tethered to God
by faith and trust.

Days

Days go marching by like soldiers on parade.
There's no good happening as far as you can see.
Your life had become nothing more than a charade.
All of your tomorrows look exactly like your yesterdays.
Joy is just a memory tucked away on some dark shelf
    of your mind,
and peace, like a long-time lover, has gone on her way,
and the despair, an unwelcome visitor, comes to the
    house of your mind and stays.

Life Is Here

Life is here. Can death be far behind? Can you feel
    his icy breath upon your neck,
feel his bony hand upon your shoulder?
No other touch is firm, no touch so colder.
Can you hear his voice, so chilling that it freezes your
    heart and mind?
Whispering in your ear, calling your name?
When he will come, no one knows, but the older we
    get, the
louder his voice becomes.
You party and you smile, you joke and you laugh
but he will come like a thief in the night and take
    away everything you have.

The Path

The path winds its way
where it leads, you do not know
but I'll walk it with you

Time Is Not Your Friend

Time is not your friend, it's an undeniable truth
it quietly steals your energy and your youth.
Time is not your friend, it knows no mercy, it knows
      no grace
it heeds no plea, but keeps on going at its own
      determined,
unhurried pace.

Donna

She goes to the window and stares out into the night,
    and what she sees fills her
heart with fright.
She knows if she goes on like this she will never last,
    because her future looks
as bleak as her past.
She thinks about the choices she made in her younger
    days and how they seemed
so right at the time.
But now she's full of questions, full of doubts, she's
    not so sure
her legacy will be a wasted life which is a crime.
Starting over again will take an awful lot of courage,
    a courage she cannot
seem to find.
She knows what she wants to be, where she wants to
    go—at least that's what she'll say.
But it's so hard to get there when you do not know
    the way

Fool's Gold

He came into your life and was exactly what you were
        looking for,
he had all the right moves, said all the right things—
        who could ask for more?
Your lonely heart sang a brand-new song, your spirit
        took off and soared,
you were afraid he'd walk away, and someone's gain
        would be your loss
so you gave him what he wanted without stopping to
        count the cost
your self-respect out the bedroom window, you tossed
But as time wore on, the thrill wore off, it grew
        quickly cold
you woke up one day feeling tired, used, and old
finding out the hard way that what you thought was
        true love
was only fool's gold.

April

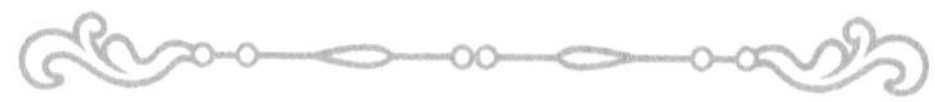

Winter goes into hibernation, and spring, in all her
    outrageous beauty,
makes her appearance.
She imparts to a weary, forlorn soul fresh hope that
    quickens my spirit again.
In the brilliant colors of the flowers, the blue sky, I
    get a foretaste of heaven.

Flakes of Snow

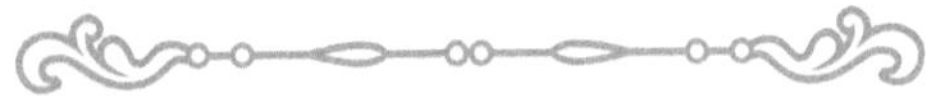

Flakes of snow parachute to earth, landing gently on
    the frozen lawn,
Like an invading army, they gather, waiting their
    marching orders.
The sun comes out and they are gone.
Our lives seem so very long, but are really like flakes
    of snow.

It's Just a Matter of Time

It's just a matter of time until the rain stops sun
    comes out again,
until I can laugh and sing once more, and the pain
    comes to an end.
It's just a matter of time until my heart is filled with
    gladness and joy,
a heart that was broken like a child's often-played-
    with toy.
It's just a matter of time until the battles I'm fighting
    will cease
Until rest and peace are finally mine

I Told You That I Loved You

I told you that I loved you, and it's just as true today
as it was all those years ago.
And nothing you can say or do will ever change that
    fact,
and that's a truth that I am sure you know.
I told you that I loved you—have I ever given you
    reason
To believe that it wasn't true?
In times of sorrow, in times of joy, was I not there
    for you?
My love was deep but not deep enough to make me
    stay
It wasn't that I wanted to leave, but you drove me
    away.
I told you that I loved you, I think you knew that
    for sure,
but you'll be back 'cos you never know what you have
until you have it no more.

Some People

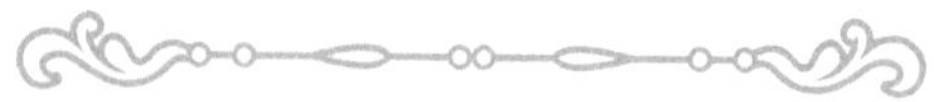

Some people are afraid to live, some are afraid to die,
some are so afraid of the truth, so they continue to be
    chained to a lie;
some people measure their lives by what they have
    gained,
some by what they have lost.
Some are afraid to look ahead, have no vision
so they remain in the past's prison.
Some seek happiness and success without counting
    the cost.
Some people hear but do not really perceive.
They do not want to understand, so they do not
    believe.
Some people look, but they do not really see
that the way things are now they will not always be.
Some people go through life with a song and a laugh
not realizing that the wind of death will come along
and blow everything
away like chaff.

My Testimony

You lifted me from the deep, dark pit and set my feet
    on solid ground,
stilled the storms of my life and made peace abound.
Put a new song in my mouth, a new joy in my heart,
took away my guilt and shame, gave me a brand-new
    start.
In my bondage, I cried out to you, and you heard
    my spirit's
desperate, quiet plea,
came down to where I was in drear and darkness,
    found and
rescued me.
Broke the bonds that held me tighter than any chain
    or rope,
set me free and gave me a new hope.

Sooner or Later

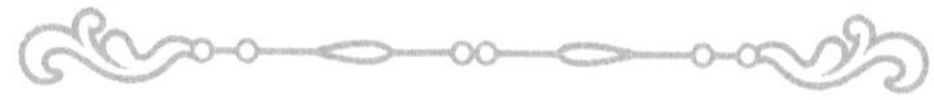

Sooner or later life intrudes, then what will you do?
Will you run and hide in your refuge, try to stay one
 step ahead?
Sooner or later fear arrives, an unwelcome guest who
refuses to leave.
Sooner or later the questions come. Hard questions,
 painful
questions, and with them, doubts.
All buzzing around in your mind like a bunch of
 mosquitoes giving you no rest.
Sooner or later, you get tired of running, tired of hid-
 ing, all your towers
Come tumbling down.
Your rose-colored glasses have broken, and you must
 face the truth.

In the Stillness

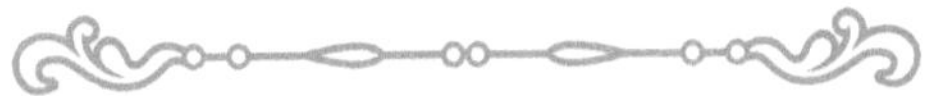

The breeze, as if confiding a secret, whispers to the
    trees
Who nod as if comprehending.
Birds speak to each other in a voice none but they
    understand
The waves of the sea rush to shore with the monoto-
    nous rhythm
taught by the ages
In the stillness of the early morning, before the world
    is awake
I meet with God, and he reassures me of his love

Missin' You Tonight

I still go to the places we used to go, still do some of
 the things we used to do
but it's not the same because you are not with me,
 and no one else will do
Loneliness is a long, long tough battle, and Lord
 knows I'm losin' the fight
Life's no longer fun because I'm missin' you tonight
In times of pain, in times of anger, you were always
 there for me with just the right actions, the
 right words
Thinkin' of spending the night with you made the
 days fly by like a flock of startled birds.
In the darkness, drear that was my life, you were the
 one bright, shining light
Now that light has gone out because I'm missin' you
 tonight.
The warmth of your body next to mine, your hair
 upon my chest,
the gentle rising, falling of your loving breast

made the night seem far too short, made everything
   all right.
Now the whole world is wrong, nothing is right
   because I'm missin' you tonight.

How?

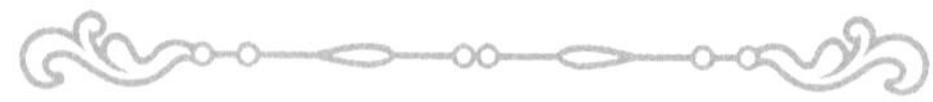

How can you fix something unless you know it's broken?

How can you understand unless a sign is given or words are spoken?

And how can you truly love with a love that's only token?

How can you enjoy the fruits of freedom when you've never known prison?

How can you know the feelings of innocence when you've outgrown 'em?

And how can you pick the flowers of true love when you've never sown the seeds?

How can you discover the answers unless you ask how, when, or why?

How can you tell a heart is aching unless you are still enough to hear it cry?

And how can you live forever unless, to self, you first die?

A Summer's Night

It's quiet. The sky is black and clear.
The stars are silver pinpoints of light
Mosquitoes buzz in my ear.
It's warm. The night is endlessly deep.
The night wraps me in its ebony arms.
A gentle breeze wanders by, passing through the trees
And my spirit is at rest and peace.

2010

Storm clouds gather in the east, there's a terrible time
    ahead.
Hearts are paralyzed by fear, minds filled with dread.
There's nowhere to run, nowhere to hide
Darkness and danger lie on every side.
Lives, like houses, lie in ruins, with no resources
To build new ones.
The winds of change are howling, they threaten
to sweep everything we knew and held dear away.
There's no place else to go, so many are forced to stay.
People find themselves left with nothing but fond
    memories
and parents will tell their children of how it used to be.
Things will never again be the way that they once were
and those in power have no good answers.

I Once Loved a Woman

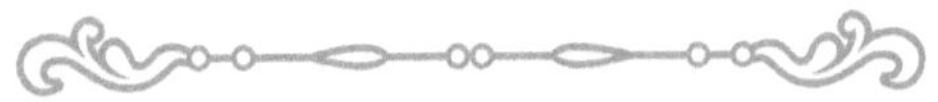

I once loved a woman, but she asked me to leave
When I asked her why, she said I lacked joie de vivre.
I said to her, "Honey, I love you," she said, "I don't
    really care
Come back to me when you get some savoir faire."
I once loved a woman beyond all reason or doubt,
She said I really didn't know what she was all about.
I once loved a woman, but she made me feel like a fool
As I walked out the door, I said, "That's not cool."
I once loved a woman, but I've learned my lesson well,
Love the wrong one, and she'll put you through hell.

The Sun

The sun poked its head through the skeletal trees as
    if trying to decide
Whether to rise or got back to bed.
It chose to rise and brighten up our day.
I was so glad to see it that I sat on my bed and cried

Life Knocked Me Down

Life knocked me down again
and I don't feel like gettin' up
It's easier to stay here on the floor
and wonder how much more I'm supposed to take.
Life knocked me down again
and I'm too tired to go on fightin'
My strength is almost gone
and my will is not my own.

Working

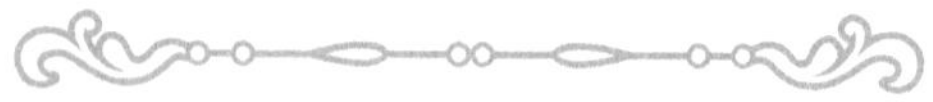

It's another morning, so after breakfast and coffee,
    it's off to
work I go
another chance to make a little dough
don't really want to do it, but there are so many people
that I owe
I could call out sick, say I stubbed my toe
but my boss would not buy my tale of woe
so it's off to work I go
how much longer I'll have to do this
I don't really know.

The Secret of Life

The secret of life, they say, is simplicity
and I was never guilty of complicity.
Never did I ever think of duplicity.
But, alas, my life never had much elasticity
which, I guess, is why I never had much felicity.

It Seems

It seems there's always another battle to be fought,
another dream to be chased,
another giant to be slain, another crisis to be faced.
It seems there's always another mountain to be
climbed, another river to be crossed,
another pain to be endured, another dream that is
lost.
It seems there's always another road to be taken,
another corner to be turned,
Another stance to be taken, another lesson to be
learned.
It seems there's always another grace to be given,
another bridge to be burned.

Everybody's Talkin'

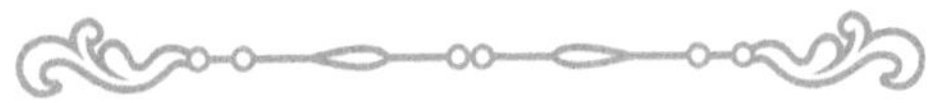

Everybody's talkin', nobody's listenin'
is it any wonder we can't hear what others have to say?
Everybody's talkin', got so much they want to say,
is it any wonder we do things our own way?
Everybody's talkin', is what we have to say as important
As what others have to say?

Hope

Hope flees, and the soul dies
Never to be revived
Hope flees, then what is left?

Time Is Short

Time is short, I hear you say
and I've got so much to do.
It seems as though I'll never get through.
I finish up one job and start another
that is new.
Time is short, and my resources are so very few.
Time is short, but if I don't do it
who will?

Marriage Gone Wrong

We sit across the table from each other, toying with
our coffee
We can't even look each other in the eye.
The silence grows more awkward as the moments go
crawling by.
Why can't we speak to each other without calling
each other names?
Or deal with each other honestly without playing
silly, stupid games?
So many years together, weathering every storm,
you'd think
That our love would only grow strong.
How could we have been so absolutely wrong?
Words that once came so easily now seem to get
caught in my throat
And smiles that warmed our times are now just
memories.
Where we go from here, it's impossible to say, 'cos
neither of us really know
'Cos we're just two people afraid to go on, too scared
to let each other go.

Like Diogenes

Like Diogenes, I searched for an honest man, but
none did I find

Though I searched all through the night and all
through the day.

I searched until I found myself on the verge of dismay.

All men, I told myself, are deceivers, liars, and cheats

There are no honest men left, I sighed

This conviction only grew as I wandered through the
streets.

I searched long and hard, I thought my search was
in vain

Then wonders of wonders, I met you, my friend.

To a Friend

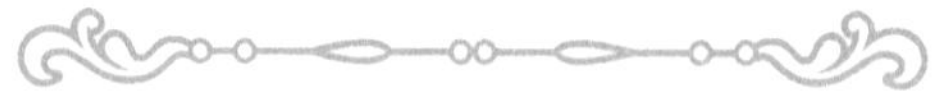

You are there for me in times of joy and in times of
    pain.
You are there for me when others are not.
You see things as they are in a way that I cannot,
Because I am too blind or simply will not.
You speak the truth even when I don't want to hear it
And even show me I have no reason to fear it.
You may wound me greatly, but it's in always love,
    now I see
I only hope I can be as good a friend to as you are
    to me.

Ode to Books

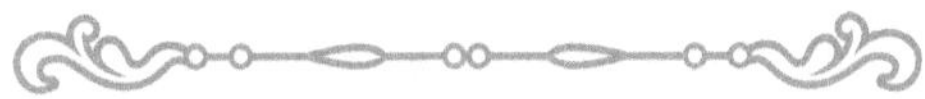

Books, books, they are wonderful tomes.
They should reside in all our homes.
They teach so much, allow the imagination to roam.
Books, books, they are friends beyond measure.
Their contents, we should eagerly devour and treasure.

An Autumn Day

White clouds slide across an azure sky
The sun is warm on my face
The wind, like a father, playfully tousles my hair
There is nowhere else that I'd rather be at this time
Than in this place
And for a while, I have no cares
Trees dressed in their royal finery of reds, yellows,
    oranges, and golds
A flotilla of leaves sail silently down the stream
To be in this place at this time never grows old
For a time I have nothing to do but sit here
And dream.

A Winter's Morn

It's a cold, dark winter's morn, and my bed feels so
good.
I don't have the will to face the day, tho' I know I
should.
The snow lies heavy on the ground, and the cares of
life
Lie heavy on my mind.
It's hard to face the future when hope has been left
behind.

Reality

Reality, like cold water on my face, brutally woke me
    to my plight
All the hopes I once held dear, like birds, suddenly
    took flight.
Reality bit me in the butt again, getting my full
    attention
I knew right then and there it was no figment of my
    imagination.

The Last Leaf of Winter

The last leaf of winter
looks old, lonely, and sad
as it clings to the skeletal arm
of the tree in front of my house.
The last leaf of winter twirls and spins
in the cold wind
holding on for dear life.

Passed By

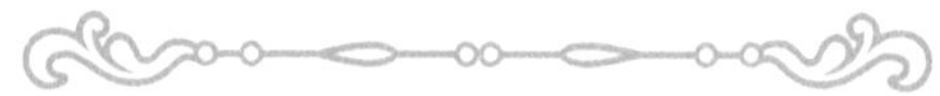

Passed by the cemetery where dreams lie buried,
searching long and hard for mine
I found the plot where they were interred
hoping they had somehow risen
but alas, they were still in the grave.
It's so damn hard to say goodbye
to them, I find.
As I left, I felt despair, for I had hoped
my dreams had somehow thrived
but to my great sadness, none had survived.

The Cross of Christ

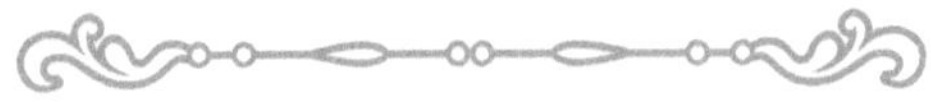

The cross of Christ. In it, I
put full faith and nothing less
The cross of Christ. To it, I cling
when drowning in a sea of stress
The cross of Christ. That instrument of pain
through that source of humiliation
salvation, full and free, I gain.
The cross of Christ. Through every trial and travail
that instrument of torture
is, for me, a source of strength
that will never fail.
The cross of Christ. That crude, old rugged tree
that instrument of death
is a source of life for me.

One Day Soon

Revelation 21:4

One day soon, the tears I shed will be tears of joy
and the dirge my heart now sings will change to
songs of eternal praise
One day soon, all of my soul-deep sighs will turn to
        laughter
and I will take part in laughter
One day soon, the groans of my imprisoned spirit
will change to shouts of victory
and I shall bask in the warmth of unconditional love.

Is It Love?

Is it love to not speak the truth even when the truth is
not what they want to hear?
Or to hold our peace out of selfishness or fear?
Is it love to simply let someone be
without hearing the Word of Life, the word that can
　　　set them free?

Tears

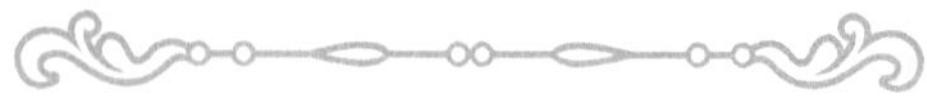

Do the tears of guilt readily flow? Tears that can
cleanse the soul.
If not, the joy of forgiveness we will never know.
Are our tears of guilt truly real?
If not, the oil of gladness we will never feel.

How Can I?

How can I describe how much you mean to me?
there aren't enough words in the universe.
You came into my life and lifted the curse.
How can I describe how much you mean to me?
Time would end before I could finish.
You fill my life with unending peace and love
that will never fade or diminish.

So I Come

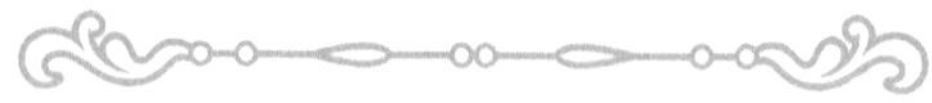

My road is long and lonely, and home seems so far
away.
The sun of hope is setting, and I cannot seem to find
my way.
My weariness is too great for me to put into words
and all my pleas for help seem to go unheard.
So I come to you in my weariness, I come to you in
my pain
and in our time alone, I find the strength to go on
again.
My road is long and lonely with many tears spilt
along the way.
At times I just need to know that things will be okay.
Fears and doubts I thought were long dead arise to
oppress and assail
and my feeble human heart begins to fail.
So I come to you with my questions, I come to you
with my tears
and in my time alone with you, I find the love that
drives out all my fears.

Nature

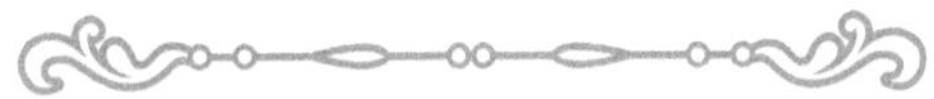

Like exquisite diamonds sitting on an ebony cushion
stars sparkle, shimmer in silent splendor.
They silently testify to the majesty of their Creator
The sun reaches up over the jade-green sea
clutching at the new day with orange fingers.
Standing on the beach in the quiet morning
I briefly glimpse the splendor of God.

The Darkness

The darkness deepens, deepens—will it ever end?
It seeps into every corner of my spirit, mind, and will.
The darkness deepens, deepens, but no matter how
deep it goes, it cannot extinguish the Light.

The Word

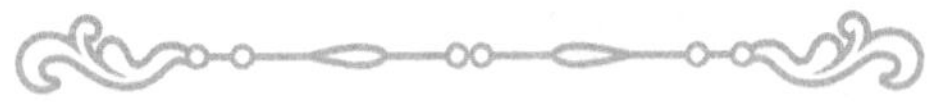

The Word of God speaks to my flagging spirit
And its strength is renewed.
The Word of God speaks to my hungry soul and
It is satisfied.
It speaks to the sickness in my life—my sick, sick life
and it is healed again and made alive.

I Found Him

I did not find him on the top of the top of the mountain
on a warm spring day
I found him in the deep, dark, valley of depression
I did not find him in the company of friends
I found him in the long, cold nights of loneliness
I did not find him on walks in the sunny parks
I found him in the storms of despair that swept into
    my life
I did not find him in the times when my strength was
    youthful and at its peak
I found him in the times my strength was gone and
    my weakness overwhelmed me

My Life

My life with sin was infected, left me feeling hope-
    less, helpless, and rejected
Came to Jesus and found myself fully accepted
Found grace and mercy—could it be? Now I am
    loved unconditionally
My life was spent trying to be good, thought if any-
    thing could save, it would
Kept on trying ever since I was a youth
Then the Holy Spirit came along and
showed me the truth
My life was full of stress, turmoil, and fear, didn't
    realize help and strength were so near
A new life I now live, a second chance I've been given
When I die, I know I'll go to heaven
Lifted me out of the darkness and the drear, showed
    me I have nothing at all to fear
turned my life upside down, when I get to heaven I'll
    receive a crown.

Voices

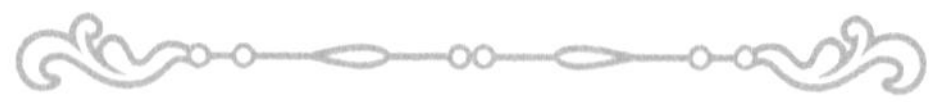

The lion of fear stands in our path, snarling and
      growling
His purpose is solely to terrorize
The soul is chilled, the mind is frozen, and the heart
is paralyzed.
He has intimidated many and will intimidate many,
      many more
but the voice of the Lamb silences the lion's roar.

We Weep Now

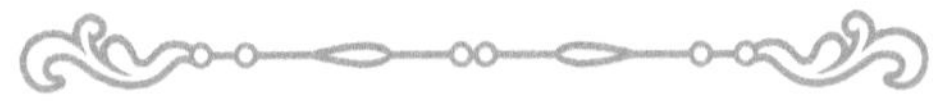

We weep now, but will rejoice later, and how great
that rejoicing will be
when Jesus and our loved ones we see.
We mourn now, but will celebrate later, and how
great that rejoicing will be!
A reunion that will last for all eternity!
No more tears, no more pain, no more loss
all because of what Jesus did on the cross.

Morality

The unborn are killed before they have a chance to
    live
The innocent die and no one even blinks an eye
Leaders lead with no thought as to what the people
    want
Their pride and arrogance are always on display.
They speak profound words but no one believes
what they say.
The way of God, they do not know, nor are they
    willing
to learn.
Defying him, mocking him, scorning him at every
    turn
What will they do as our nation burns?
But God is watching, watching, silently, patiently
    waiting
as our nation piles up its sins.
We are in a war with God, a war we cannot hope to
    win.

If I Chose the Road

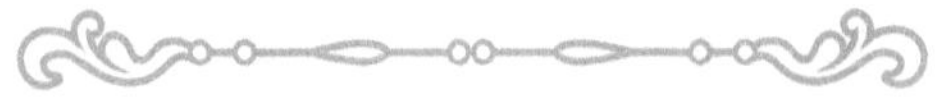

If I chose the road I had to walk, it would not be the
     one I'm on
It would be broad and smooth, requiring no faith,
     no trust.
But God chose my road long ago even before I was
     born.
A narrow road with potholes, a road leading through
     the valley
deep and dark.
A road of loneliness, a road of pain, a road of doubt
     and fear, a road I would not have taken on my
     own.
If I chose the road, it would not have ended well, it
     would run past the cross
and straight into hell.
But God chose my road out of all of them, the road
     that leads
me to the New Jerusalem

Questions

How do you fill a leaky cup? Or revive a long-lost
　　dream?
How do you put toothpaste back in the tube?
Or autumn leaves back on the trees?
How do you read when there are no words on the
　　page?
Or hear when there is no sound?
How do you see clearly when there is no light?

The Road

We walked the road hand in hand for forty-plus years
The journey filled with laughter, struggle, and tears
I thought we would walk it for many more, but I was
wrong, for God had other plans.
Now for the foreseeable future, I will be walking the
    road alone
but I know Jesus and Joyce'll be waiting for me when
    I finally
make it home.

One Day Closer

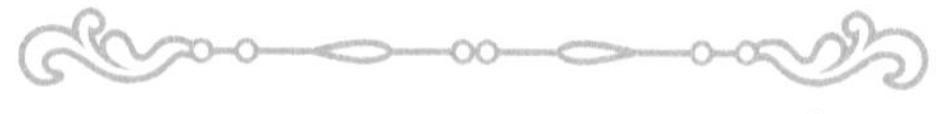

Went to bed last night worried and in distress
for the nation I love is in terrible distress.
But I awoke this morning, and joy in my heart did burn
for I realized we were one day closer to Jesus's return.
One day closer to hope fulfilled,
the voice of the devil forever stilled.
One day closer to promises kept,
at the thought of being with my Savior
my heart, like a lamb, leapt.
One day closer to the end of labor and toil,
the end of sorrow and pain.
One day closer to paradise regained.

Once I Was

Once I was helpless, now I have unfailing help
in making it through the dark and lonely nights.
Once I was hopeless, now I have hope
That, like the summer sun, shines bright
and carries me through the toughest times of my life.
Once I was blind, but now I clearly see
and it's all because of Calvary's tree.
Once I was hurting, but now I am healed.
Once I was lost, but now I am sealed.
Once I was imprisoned, but now I am free,
and it's all because of Calvary's tree.

So I Turn to You, Jesus

There are nights that are dark and silent, when sleep
    just will not come
because my mind is churning like the sea in a storm.
There are days that are long and tough and seem as if
    they'll never end
'cos things haven't gone my way.
There are times I get so far down that it seems I'll
    never be up again.
My mind clouds over with doubt and weariness like
    the sky on a winter's day.
There are times when I wonder if it's all been worth
    it.
It feels like all my work's been in vain.
After all the toil, tears, and sacrifice, what has been
    gained?
So I turn to you, Jesus, I turn to you, and in that time
I find the rest my weary soul desperately craves.
So I turn to you, Jesus, I turn to you, and in the qui-
    etness I find
the strength I do not have.
Days come along when I ask myself, "What's the use?
Why keep on trying? All I can ever do is lose."

I do not feel like going on, all I do is make excuses
so I turn to you, Jesus, I turn to you, and find the
     courage I do
not possess.

I Came to Him

I came to him needy and left satisfied
came to him in pain and sickness and left healed.
I came to him steeped in sin, shame, and guilt
and left restored and forgiven,
I came to him lonely and deeply confused
and left loved unconditionally.
I came to him disheartened and discouraged
and left full of hope.
I came to him with all my frailty and unworthiness
and found total acceptance, nothing less.

I Will Praise You, O Lord

When your goodness is hidden from my desperately
      seeking eye
like the sun on a cloudy day
and faith is hard to come by and giants are standing
      in my way
When I cannot hold my ground because the odds
      against me are too great
and I feel as though I can no longer stand
My foes are too many to even contemplate
I cannot see your face or feel your loving, powerful
      hand
I will praise you, O Lord, because I don't know what
      else to do
When my thoughts turn to the mistakes and errors
      of my past
My prayers feel like they're not breaking through
because the ceiling's turned to brass

When your blessings that once flowed now seem to
      have all dried up
I will praise you, O Lord, because I don't know what
      else to do.

When the long-time job goes south, leaving me behind
and chances of finding another are slim to none
When worry seeps into my mind because I don't
    know what
the future holds,
I will praise you for who you are and all that you have
    done
When there's no money in the bank and the bills are
    coming due
I will praise you, O Lord, because I don't know what
    else to do
When things aren't going my way and it seems as if
    they never will again
and the bluebird of happiness has flown, never to
    return
I find myself longing for things the way they once
    were
When all of the things for which I've worked and
    planned have turned
to dust
and my dreams once bright and shiny have become
    coated with rust
and things are so bad I don't know whether to laugh
    or cry or how I'll
make it through
I will praise you, O Lord, because I don't know what
    else to do

You Were There All the Time

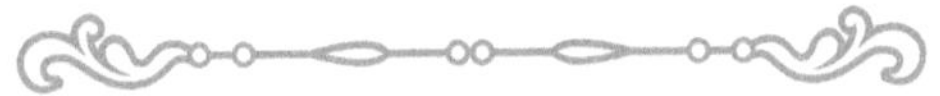

You were there all the time, it was just that I could
    never
see my need for you.
I thought I could handle life all by myself.
Wanted to call the shots, be my own boss
made decisions blithely, not counting the cost
You were there all the time, waiting quietly for me
    to come
to the end of my resources
You were there all the time, watching like a father
    looking out the window
ready to come to my aid at a moment's notice.
You were there all the time, waiting, waiting patiently
knowing that I would eventually come running to you
like a hurt child.
You were there all the time, and I am now glad you
    were.

If

(Psalm 36:5–6)

If the sky had an end, so would God's faithfulness
If the mountains could be removed, so could God's
justice and righteousness.
If time had an end and the earth ceased to turn,
so would God's love.

Taking the Road Less Traveled

Taking the road less traveled—what is it I will find?
Wonders too great to explain?
Miracles to which I've been previously blind?
Taking the road less traveled—who is it I'll meet?
The man I used to be or the man I want to be?
More amazing victories or more discouraging defeats?

I Faced Fear Today

(1 John 4:18)

I faced fear today with all its ugliness
and bravado.
It tried to scare me and make me fret.
I faced fear today, and it tried to convince me
that you just didn't care.
I faced fear today with a lot of prayer and praise.
I faced fear today, and he backed down.

I Am His

I am his, and he is mine
held together by a love divine.

I am his, and he is mine,
He deigns to call me friend.
I am his, and he is mine.
In him, everything I need, I find.

The Soldier

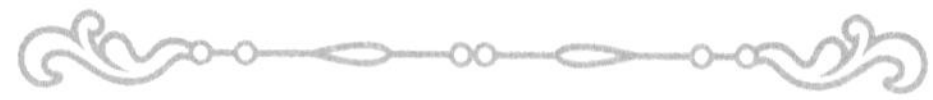

I'm heading home, my face turned to the setting sun.
The battle was hard and really not much fun.
But in my mind's eye, I can plainly see,
the ones I love watching eagerly for me.
The battle has been long, the battle has been hard,
and rest for me was not really in the cards.
But with my shield upon my back and my sword
strapped to my side,
Battered and scarred, I press on,
knowing at home I'll forever abide.

Speaking with God

Speaking with God today about all the things he wanted me to do.
Feeling overwhelmed, I thought there's no way.
I told him, "Lord, I can't do this, I'm just a man."
He said, "I know you can't, just believe that I can."

I Used To

I used to ask God why
And sit hours waiting for his reply.
It was oh so tough waiting.
Then he said, "You don't need to know
I do, and that's enough."

If I Had Wings

If I had wings, I'd soar high above
The absurdity of life, away from
Anxiety, fear, and strife.
If I had wings, I'd fly away and, at last
Be at rest in a place where life can no
Longer molest.

About the Author

Russell Topping was born and still lives in Lambertville, New Jersey with his comfort buddy Emerson the cat.

Having graduated in 1964 from high school he went right into the workforce, working in the advertising department of the local newspaper, a distribution center, Home Depot, a Certified Nursing Assistant, and a food store clerk before retiring in 2014.

A widower, he has been volunteering at Tabby' Place, a sanctuary-free, no kill cat sanctuary in nearby Ringoes.

He spends most of his spare time fly fishing and is into photography.